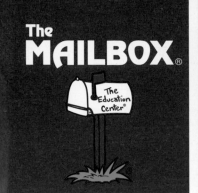

The MAILBOX®

The Education Center®

Centers From A to Z

grades PreK-K

S0-AYE-791

More Than 180 Alphabet Activities for Popular Learning Centers

- Art center
- Block center
- Dramatic-play area
- Fine-motor area
- Flannelboard center
- Games center
- Gross-motor area
- Literacy center
- Math center
- Play dough center
- Puzzle center
- Sand table
- Sensory center
- Snack center
- Water table
- Writing center

Managing Editor: Kelly Robertson

Editorial Team: Becky S. Andrews, Randi Austin, Diane Badden, Amy Brinton, Tricia Brown, Kimberley Bruck, Karen A. Brudnak, Marie E. Cecchini, Pam Crane, Roxanne LaBell Dearman, Beth Deki, Shanda Fitte, Ada Goren, Heather E. Graley, Tazmen Hansen, Marsha Heim, Lori Z. Henry, Lucia Kemp Henry, Kim Hintze, Debra Liverman, Kitty Lowrance, Coramarie Marinan, Brenda Miner, Jennifer Nunn, Tina Petersen, Gerri Primak, Mark Rainey, Greg D. Rieves, Hope Rodgers, Rebecca Saunders, Betty Silkunas, Leanne Stratton Swinson, Donna K. Teal, Rachael Traylor, Sharon M. Tresino, Carole Watkins, Zane Williard, Virginia Zeletzki

www.themailbox.com

Printed in the United States
10 9 8 7 6 5 4 3 2 1

HPS 215494

Table of Contents

What's Inside

Center activities for **every** alphabet letter!

Mm

Literacy Center

Place in a container several objects or pictures of objects whose names begin with /m/. Add a few items whose names begin with different sounds as well. Display the container near a large moon-shaped cutout. A child puts each item whose name begins like *moon* on top of the cutout. **Beginning sound /m/**

Play Dough Center

Set out play dough, pipe cleaner pieces, and a laminated copy of page 104. A child molds dough into a mouse shape and adds a pipe cleaner tail. He moves the mouse along the *M*, from the mouse hole to the muffin. Then he pretends to have the mouse eat the muffin as he says, "Munch, munch, munch—/m/, /m/, good!" emphasizing each /m/ sound. **Letter-sound association**

Mouse Maze

52

Mm Mm Mm Mm Mm Mm Mm Mm Mm

Centers From A to Z • ©The Mailbox® Books • TEC61277

Qq

Water Table

Float several rubber ducks in your water table. Provide a spray bottle filled with water. A child uses the spray bottle to squirt the ducks. Each time he squirts a duck, he says, "Quack, quack!" emphasizing the beginning sounds. **Beginning sound /kw/**

Literacy Center

Store several letter *Q* manipulatives in a bag. Add a few different letter manipulatives as well. Place the bag near a small quilt. A youngster picks a letter from the bag. If it is a letter *Q*, he places it on the quilt. If it is not, he sets the letter aside. He continues until the bag is empty. **Letter recognition**

68

Qq Qq Qq Qq Qq Qq Qq Qq Qq

Centers From A to Z • ©The Mailbox® Books • TEC61277

Patterns and More

Ee Elephant and Peanut Patterns
Use with "Literacy Center" on page 22.

100

Centers From A to Z • ©The Mailbox® Books • TEC61277

I Spy the Letter I

P	I	O	m
i	A	I	s
i	I	G	i
c	I	F	z
I	I	I	d
O	I	I	d

102   Note to the teacher: Use with "Math Center" on page 36.

Centers From A to Z • ©The Mailbox® Books • TEC61277

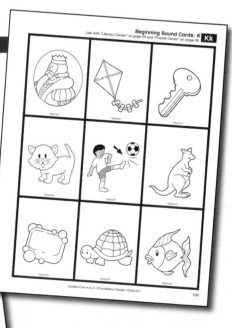

Beginning Sound Cards: K   Kk
Use with "Literacy Center" on page 44 and "Puzzle Center" on page 45.

103   *Centers From A to Z • ©The Mailbox® Books • TEC61277*

Literacy Center

Place an apron with a pocket near small objects or pictures of objects that begin with /ā/, along with a few objects or pictures of objects that begin with other letters. A child puts on the apron and places the objects that begin like *apron* in the pockets. **Beginning sound /ā/**

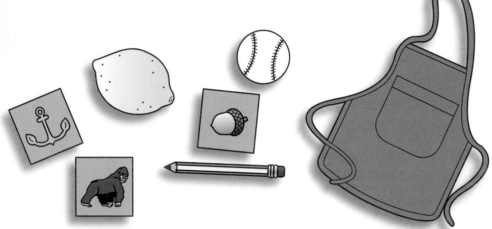

Art Center

For each child, program a sheet of paper with the sentence starter shown. Set out the programmed papers, gray construction paper ape head cutouts, a shallow container of black paint, a sponge, and crayons. A child sponge-paints around the edge of the ape head. When the paint is dry, she uses crayons to add facial details. Then she glues her ape to a paper and completes the sentence. **Letter-sound association**

Ape starts with A .

Attach a strip of masking tape to a surface and label it as shown. Then cut out several green copies of the alligator patterns on page 96. Place the alligators near the tape strip. A child reads the letters on the strip and places a matching alligator above each letter to create a pattern. **Letter matching**

To make a batch of alphabet soup, float foam letters in your water table. Be sure to include several letter *A*s. A little one stirs the soup with a plastic slotted spoon. Then he scoops out each letter *A* and places it in a plastic bowl. **Letter recognition**

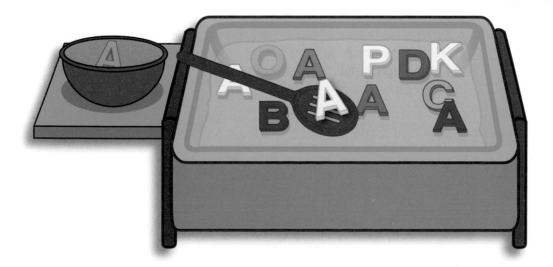

Play Dough Center

On a large paper tree, write several *A*s and a few distracter letters. Place red, yellow, and green play dough near the tree. A child reads each letter on the tree. Then she rolls pieces of play dough into balls so they look like apples and places an apple on each *A*. **Letter recognition**

Games Center

Make several acorn cutouts (pattern on page 96). On each acorn, write either an uppercase or a lowercase *A*. Place the acorns in a facedown stack near two baskets that are labeled as shown. Each player takes an acorn in turn. He reads the letter and places the acorn in the matching basket. **Uppercase and lowercase letters**

Centers From A to Z • ©The Mailbox® Books • TEC61277

Make several ant cutouts (pattern on page 96) and write either an uppercase or a lowercase *A* on each. Spread a blanket on the floor and scatter the ants on the blanket. Set a picnic basket nearby. A child reads the letter on each ant. If the ant is labeled with *A*, she places it in the basket. If it's labeled with *a*, she leaves it on the blanket. **Uppercase and lowercase letters**

(pattern on page 96)

Literacy Center

Fine-Motor Area

On a sheet of paper, draw a large *A* and copy the paper to make a class supply. Then set out the copies along with a squeeze bottle of glue, silver glitter, crayons, and markers. A child decorates the *A* so it looks like an angel. Then he squeezes glue along the *A* and sprinkles glitter on the glue. Finally, he shakes off the excess glitter. **Letter formation**

Snack Center

Set out large and small bear cookie cutters, bread slices, whipped butter, paper towels, and plastic knives. A child presses each cookie cutter into a bread slice to make a big bear and a baby bear. Then he spreads butter on each bear as he says the words *big bear, baby bear,* and *butter,* emphasizing each /b/ sound. **Sound awareness of /b/**

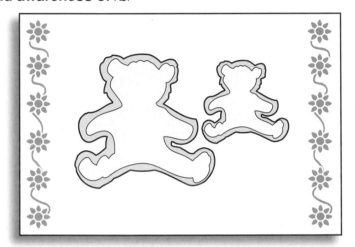

Literacy Center

Gather several items whose names begin with /b/. Also provide a few items whose names begin with different sounds. Display an empty backpack near the items. A little one packs the backpack with each item whose name begins like *backpack.* **Beginning sound /b/**

Games Center

Make a tagboard bus like the one shown; then cut out a copy of the cards on page 97. Program the backs of the cards to make them self-checking and arrange them faceup. A youngster points to a card, determines if the pictured item begins with /b/, and checks his answer. If the pictured item begins with /b/, he places it on the bus. If it does not, he returns it faceup with the remaining cards. The next child takes a turn in the same way. Alternate play continues until each card whose pictured item begins with /b/ has been placed on the bus. **Beginning sound /b/**

Flannelboard Center

Cut an equal number of *B*s and butterfly bodies from felt. A child puts a butterfly body on the board. Then he chooses a *B*, says its name and beginning sound, and aligns the straight edge of the letter with the body of the butterfly. He repeats the process to make more butterflies. **Letter-sound association**

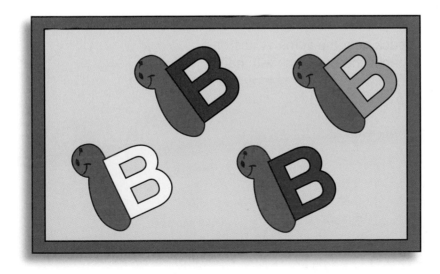

Block Center

Label each of several blocks with an uppercase *B*. Label a few more blocks with different uppercase letters. Display a large *B* in the area. A child looks for the blocks labeled with a *B* and uses them to build a structure of his own design. **Letter recognition**

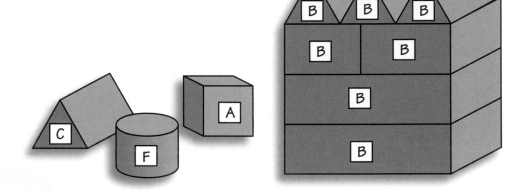

Gross-Motor Area

Label each of a supply of balls with either an uppercase *B* or a lowercase *b*. Store the balls in a container. Several feet away, place two empty boxes labeled as shown. A student takes a ball and tosses it in the box labeled with the matching letter. He continues with each remaining ball. **Uppercase and lowercase letters**

Centers From A to Z • ©The Mailbox® Books • TEC61277

Puzzle Center

Cut several large *B*s from different-colored sheets of craft foam. Puzzle-cut each letter; then put each puzzle in a separate resealable plastic bag. Also display a large tagboard *B*. A child removes the pieces from a bag and assembles the letter, using the tagboard *B* as a guide. **Letter formation**

Writing Center

Pour a batch of pureed berries into an ice cube tray. Insert a craft stick in each section and then place the tray in a freezer. For each child, label a sheet of paper with the letter *B*. A student uses a frozen berry pop to practice writing the letter *B*. **Letter formation**

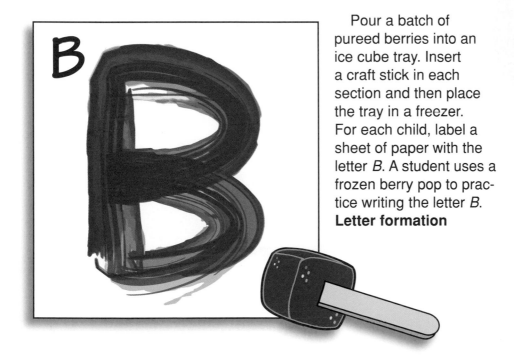

Literacy Center

Place inside a plastic cookie jar several objects or pictures of objects whose names begin with the hard *c* sound. Also add a few items whose names begin with different sounds. Place the jar near a large cookie cutout. A child removes each item from the jar and puts each one whose name begins like *cookie* on the cutout. **Beginning sound /k/**

Play Dough Center

Set out play dough, cupcake liners, and letter *C* manipulatives. A youngster molds play dough into cupcake shapes and puts each one in a liner. Then he decorates the cupcakes with *C*s as he repeats the word *cupcake*. **Letter-sound association**

Centers From A to Z • ©The Mailbox® Books • TEC61277

Fine-Motor Area

For each child, cut the front panel from a paper shopping bag and program it as shown. Provide catalogs, grocery circulars, scissors, and glue. A student cuts out pictures of items whose names begin with the hard *c* sound and then glues them to the panel. **Letter-sound association**

Dramatic-Play Area

To create a campsite, build a makeshift fire using cardboard tubes and orange tissue paper. Provide camping-related items along with a skillet; a spatula; and a small cooler that contains an assortment of letter manipulatives, including several *C*s. A child uses the spatula to place each *C* in the skillet and then pretends to cook the letters over the fire. **Letter recognition**

Sensory Center

Make a copy of page 98. Cut out the patterns and then tape each cutout to a separate container. Spread green paper shreds (grass) in your sensory table and then hide die-cut uppercase and lowercase *C*s under the grass. A student searches through the grass to find each *C* and places it in the appropriate container. **Uppercase and lowercase letters**

Art Center

For each child, program a sheet of paper with a letter *C* outline. Set out shallow containers of different paint colors and provide a cork for each color. A student fills an outline with colorful cork prints by dipping one end of a cork in paint and then pressing it repeatedly on the paper. She continues making prints, switching corks and paint colors as desired, until the outline is filled. **Letter formation**

Centers From A to Z • ©The Mailbox® Books • TEC61277

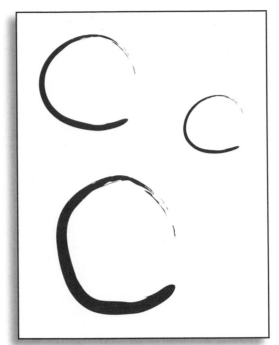

Combine instant coffee and water to make a dark, richly scented watercolor paint. Set out paper and paintbrushes and display a large *C*. A student sniffs the aroma of the coffee as he paints *C*s on the paper. **Letter formation**

Sensory Center

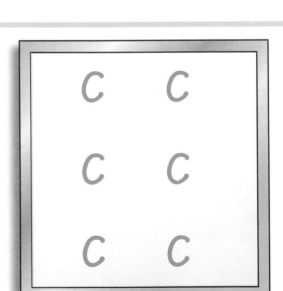

For this counting activity, set out student whiteboards, colorful dry-erase markers, and a large die. Display a large *C*. A student rolls the die and counts aloud the number of dots on top. Then he chooses a marker color and writes the corresponding number of *C*s. He repeats the activity one more time using a different marker color. For a partner activity, students take an equal number of turns. Then each child counts the total number of *C*s he wrote and the partners compare their results. **Letter formation**

Math Center

Play Dough Center

Set out different colors of play dough and clean box lids (or doughnut boxes). A youngster molds a variety of doughnut shapes and puts them inside a box lid. Then she announces, "Doughnuts for delivery!" emphasizing each /d/ sound. **Beginning sound /d/**

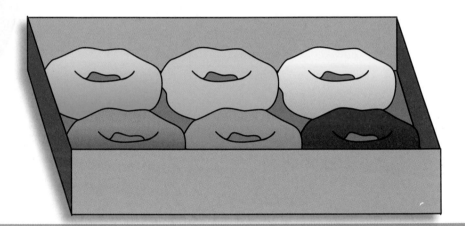

Games Center

Turn a box upside down and cut a door in one side. Put in the box a variety of objects, some whose names begin with /d/ and some whose names do not. Place a large diamond-shape cutout near the box. A child removes an item through the door and places it on the cutout if its name begins like *diamond.* If it does not, he places the item to the side. The next child takes a turn and play continues in the same way with each remaining object. **Beginning sound /d/**

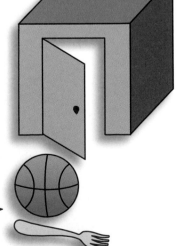

Art Center

For each child, cut out a large tagboard *D*. Set out craft items—such as craft foam shapes, die-cut shapes, and stickers—that picture objects whose names begin with /d/. Also provide glue. A youngster chooses an item, says its name and its beginning sound, and then attaches the item to her letter cutout. She continues in the same way, decorating her cutout with a variety of items whose names begin with /d/. **Letter-sound association**

Sensory Center

Fill your sensory table with potting soil and bury several plastic *D*s and a handful of other letters in the dirt. Also provide garden gloves, a plastic shovel, and a dump truck labeled with the letter *D*. A child digs for *D*s in the dirt. When she finds one, she puts it in the dump truck. As she digs, she repeats the phrase "digging for *D*s in the dirt," emphasizing each /d/ sound. **Letter recognition**

Literacy Center

Make student copies of the dog on page 99. Label a card with an uppercase and a lowercase *D*, making each letter a different color. Set out the card and a bingo dauber for each color used. A student refers to the card and presses the appropriate dauber color onto the corresponding letters on the dog pattern. **Uppercase and lowercase letters**

D Is for *Dog*

Dramatic-Play Area

To make a doggy day care, provide stuffed toy dogs, two dog bowls labeled as shown, and other dog-related items. Label a supply of tagboard dog bones with either an uppercase or a lowercase *D*. If desired, store the bones in an empty dog-treat box. When it's feeding time, a youngster puts each bone in the bowl labeled with its matching letter. Then he pretends to feed the dogs at the day care. **Uppercase and lowercase letters**

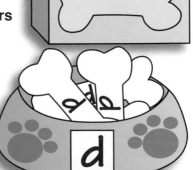

Centers From A to Z • ©The Mailbox® Books • TEC61277

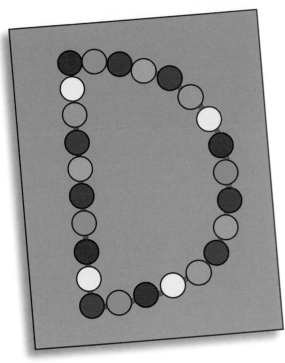

Fine-Motor Area

For each child, write a large *D* on a sheet of paper. Set out colorful sticky dots. A student presses a series of dots along the lines of the letter. When she is finished, she uses her pointer finger to trace and feel the shape of her dotted *D.* **Letter formation**

Writing Center

Put a layer of dirt in a shallow container. Supply a small wooden dowel, a hand rake (or something similar), and an example of an uppercase and a lowercase *D.* A child uses the dowel to write each letter in the dirt. Then he uses the rake to smooth out the dirt. He continues in the same way to practice writing the letters. **Letter formation**

Math Center

Gather several dominoes that have sections with equal numbers of dots and a few dominoes that have sections with unequal numbers. Program a sheet of paper like the one shown. A youngster counts the dots on each section of a domino. If the domino has sections with equal numbers of dots, he places it on the paper as he says the word *equal,* emphasizing the long *e* sound. **Beginning sound /ē/**

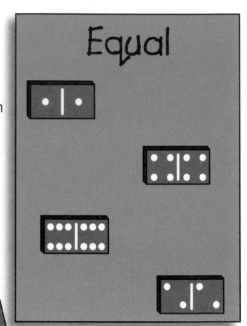

Literacy Center

Label each of several cards with *E* or *e*. For each card, program an envelope with a matching letter. Set out the cards and the envelopes. A child reads the letter on each card and places it in a matching envelope. **Letter matching**

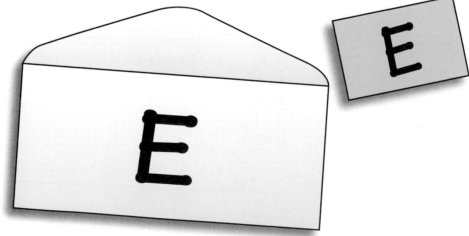

Centers From A to Z • ©The Mailbox® Books • TEC61277

Snack Center

Set out bread slices, paper plates, a plastic knife, and a topping such as whipped butter or cream cheese. Also display a large letter *E* cutout. A little one places a slice of bread on a plate and uses the plastic knife to cut an uppercase *E* from the bread. As she works, she says, "*E*s are easy to make," emphasizing each long *e* sound. Then she spreads some topping on the *E* and eats her snack. **Letter-sound association**

Games Center

For this partner game, set out a large eagle cutout like the one shown. Near the cutout place a face-down stack of letter cards containing several cards labeled with *E*. To play, each child takes a card, in turn, and reads the letter. If the card is labeled with an *E*, he places it on the eagle as he says, "An *E* for *eagle!*" If the card is labeled with a different letter, he places it in a discard pile. Alternate play continues until each letter card has been sorted. **Letter recognition**

Literacy Center

Write an uppercase or lowercase *E* on each of several copies of a peanut pattern from page 100. Label two copies of the elephant pattern from the same page, as shown, and set the peanuts nearby. A child "feeds" each peanut to the matching elephant. **Uppercase and lowercase letters**

Literacy Center

Program one half of each of 12 plastic eggs with an uppercase *E* and the other half of each egg with a lowercase *e*. Then separate the eggs and set the halves near a sanitized egg carton. A youngster puts matching egg halves together and places each whole egg in the carton. **Uppercase and lowercase letters**

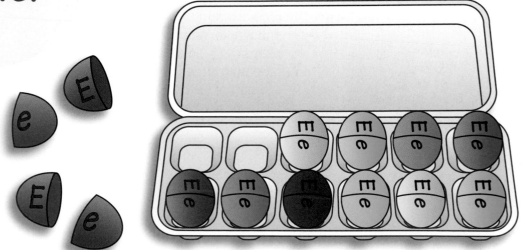

Centers From A to Z • ©The Mailbox® Books • TEC61277

Set out tagboard egg tracers, paper, a pencil, and crayons. A child traces several eggs on her paper and writes an uppercase or lowercase *E* in each egg. Then she chooses the egg that displays her best handwriting and decorates it as desired. **Letter formation**

Fine-Motor Area

For each child, clip a large sheet of paper on an easel. Set cups of colorful paints and paintbrushes nearby. A child paints several uppercase *E*s and lowercase *e*'s on the paper. As she works, she says, "I am painting *E*s on the easel," emphasizing each long *e* sound. When she is satisfied with her work, she unclips the paper from the easel and sets it aside to dry. **Letter formation**

Art Center

Ff

Art Center

Set out a feather cutout, paint, and a large craft feather. A child uses the feather to paint the cutout. As she paints, she practices the initial sound of *feather* by making the /f/ sound each time she strokes the feather on the cutout. **Beginning sound /f/**

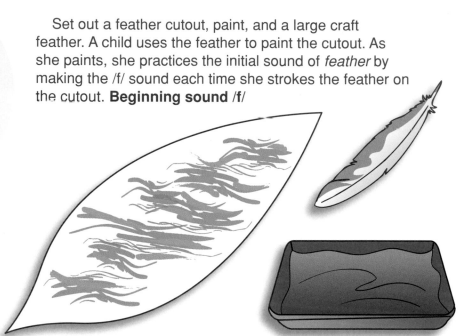

Dramatic-Play Area

Mount to a wall a sheet of poster board trimmed to resemble flames. Place near the flames several objects or pictures of objects whose names begin with /f/ and a few objects whose names begin with different sounds. Also provide a plastic firefighter helmet. A youngster puts on the helmet and pretends to be a firefighter as he moves objects whose name begins like *fire* away from the flames. **Beginning sound /f/**

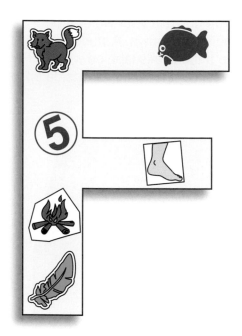

Art Center

Cut out a construction paper *F* for each child. Set out items that have pictures whose names begin with /f/, such as stickers, stampers, and images from magazines. Also provide ink pads and glue. A student picks an item, says its name and its beginning sound, and then glues, sticks, or stamps the item on his letter cutout. He continues in the same way, decorating his cutout with a variety of items whose names begin with /f/. **Letter-sound association**

Gross-Motor Area

Use masking tape to make an oversize *F* on the floor. Place near the letter objects that begin with /f/, as shown. A youngster walks along the letter, making the /f/ sound as she walks. When she reaches an object, she says its name—emphasizing its beginning sound—and then continues walking in the same way. She repeats the activity several times by hopping, crawling, and tiptoeing on the letter. **Letter-sound association**

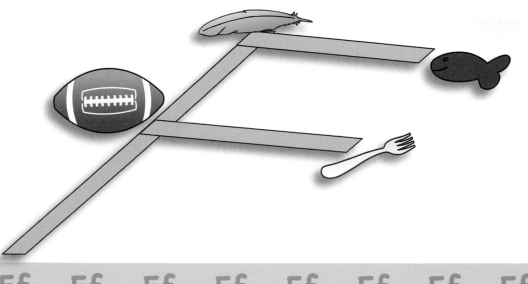

Water Table

Label several craft foam fish—some with *F*s and a few with different letters. Float the fish letter side down in your water table. Provide a small fishnet and a pail labeled as shown. A student uses the net to scoop a fish from the water. If the fish is labeled with an *F*, he places it in the pail. If not, he returns it to the water letter side up.

Block Center

Label a sheet of poster board with a large uppercase *F*. Set out a variety of rectangular blocks. A child arranges blocks on top of the labeled poster board to form the letter. Then she uses more blocks to practice making the letter next to the poster board. **Letter formation**

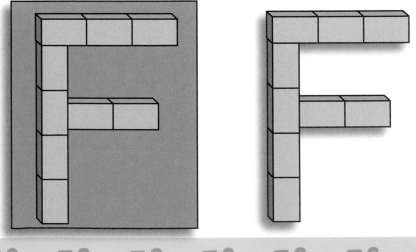

Centers From A to Z • ©The Mailbox® Books • TEC61277

Post the letter *F* and provide a sheet of construction paper, a container of fingerpaint, and a small foam football. A child fingerpaints the paper. Then he uses the foam football to write *F*s in the wet paint. **Letter formation**

Writing Center

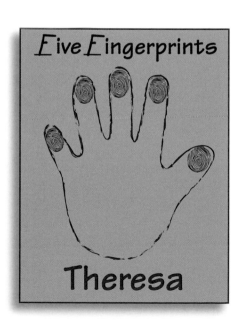

For this one-to-one correspondence center, label for each child a sheet of paper with the words shown, inserting a blank space for each *F*. Set out ink pads and markers. A child traces her hand on a paper and counts her fingers. Next, she presses each fingertip on an ink pad and then onto the corresponding fingertip of her tracing, matching one to one. She counts the fingerprints aloud and then writes an *F* in each blank space to complete the words. **For an added challenge,** have students complete the activity with three hand tracings and fifteen fingerprints. **Letter formation**

Math Center

Sand Table

Place garden-themed props—such as plastic tools, silk or paper flowers, and empty seed packets—near the sand table. A child uses the props to create a garden. While he is gardening, he recites, "This will be a gorgeous garden," emphasizing each hard /g/ sound. **Beginning sound /g/**

Literacy Center

Set out several objects or pictures of objects whose names begin with the hard /g/ sound, along with a few items whose names begin with other sounds. Place a gift bag nearby. A child puts in the bag each item whose name begins like *gift*. **Beginning sound /g/**

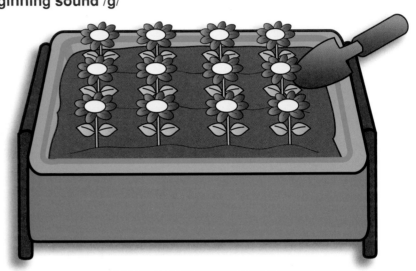

Games Center

To prepare this partner center, set out five disposable cups and a letter *G* manipulative. Player 1 places the cups in a row upside down. He hides the letter under one of the cups and then rearranges the order of the cups. Player 2 picks up cups until he finds the hidden letter. When the letter's location is revealed, each player names a word that begins with the hard /g/ sound. Then the partners switch roles and play another round. **Letter-sound association**

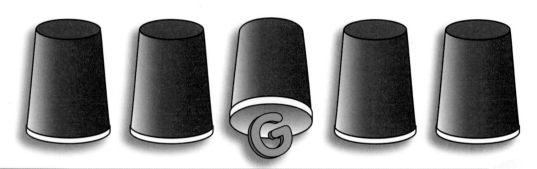

Gross-Motor Area

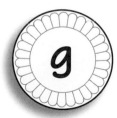

Label each of several paper plates with an uppercase or a lowercase *G*. For each plate, attach a matching letter card to a beanbag. Randomly arrange the plates on the floor and set the beanbags nearby. A child tosses each beanbag onto a plate with a matching letter. **Letter matching**

Literacy Center

Prepare a large paper gumball machine like the one shown. Then write an uppercase or a lowercase *G* on each of several colorful paper circles (gumballs). On a few other gumballs, write letters other than *G*. Set all the gumballs near the gumball machine. A child places the gumballs with uppercase or lowercase *G*s on the gumball machine and sets the other gumballs aside. **Letter recognition**

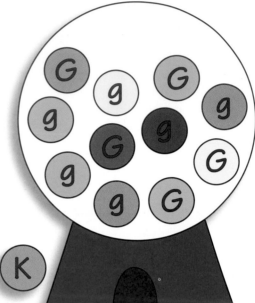

Flannelboard Center

Label two bowl cutouts as shown. Then write an uppercase or a lowercase *G* on each of a supply of gumdrop cutouts. Prepare the cutouts for flannelboard use. Then attach the bowls to the flannelboard and set the gumdrops nearby. A child sticks each gumdrop to the board above its matching candy bowl. **Uppercase and lowercase letters**

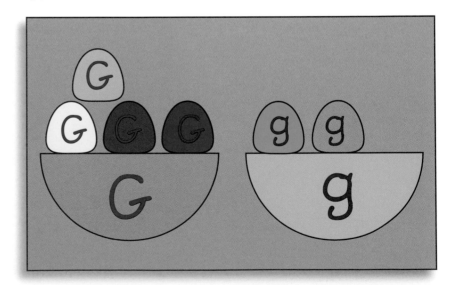

Centers From A to Z • ©The Mailbox® Books • TEC61277

Spray-paint a supply of small rocks gold. When the paint is dry, label each rock with an uppercase or a lowercase *G*. Bury the rocks in a tub filled with rice. A child uses his hands to dig in the rice to find gold. Then he sorts the gold into two groups: uppercase and lowercase *G*s. **Uppercase and lowercase letters**

Sensory Center

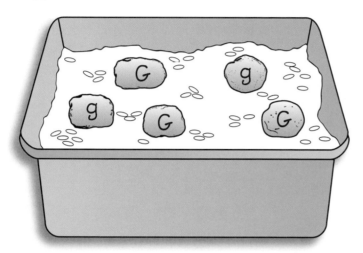

For each child, program a small paper plate like the one shown. Also provide fish-shaped crackers. A child places the crackers end to end to form the letters on his plate. When he has finished, he nibbles on the crackers. **Letter formation**

Snack Center

Centers From A to Z • ©The Mailbox® Books • TEC61277

Gross-Motor Area

Place a plastic hoop on the floor. A child hops inside the hoop as she recites the chant shown, emphasizing each /h/ sound. Then she hops outside the hoop and repeats the chant with the appropriate positional word. **Beginning sound /h/**

I am hop, hop, hopping [inside] the hoop.

Block Center

Color and cut apart a copy of the picture cards on page 101. Attach each card to a cube-shaped block (bale of hay) and place the bales in a container. Set out the container and a toy horse or a picture of a horse. A youngster names the picture on a bale of hay and places it near the horse if it begins like *hay*. **Beginning sound /h/**

Label a supply of paper hearts each with an upper-case or lowercase *H* and laminate them for durability. Bury the hearts in the sand and set plastic digging tools nearby. A student digs in the sand to hunt for the hearts. As he digs, he recites, "I am a happy heart hunter," emphasizing each /h/ sound. **Letter-sound association**

Sand Table

Program blank cards with letters, making sure several cards are labeled with *H*s. Also provide a hat. A youngster reads the letter on each card. He places the *H* cards in the hat and the other cards beside the hat. **Letter recognition**

Literacy Center

Games Center

For this partner game, set out a large owl cutout. Near the cutout place a facedown stack of letter cards containing several cards labeled with *H*. To play, each child takes a card in turn and reads the letter. If the card is labeled with an *H*, he places it on the owl and says, "Hoot, hoot!" If the card is labeled with a different letter, he sets it aside. Alternate play continues until each letter card has been sorted. **Letter recognition**

Literacy Center

Label two house cutouts as shown. Set the houses near several uppercase and lowercase letter *H* manipulatives. A child places each letter manipulative on the appropriate house. **Uppercase and lowercase letters**

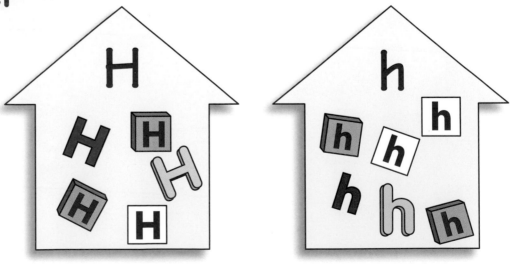

Writing Center

For each child, set out two hand cutouts, a sheet of construction paper, markers, and glue. A child writes uppercase *H*s on one cutout and lowercase *h*'s on the other cutout. Then he glues the cutouts to a sheet of paper as shown. **Letter formation**

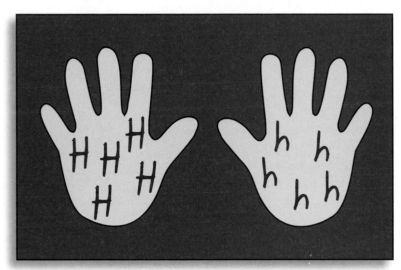

Fine-Motor Center

Set out a hexagon-shaped block, blank paper, and colored pencils. On a sheet of paper, a child makes several connected tracings of the hexagon so the tracings form a honeycomb. Then he writes an uppercase or lowercase *H* in each honeycomb cell. **Letter formation**

Art Center

Set out construction paper, ice cream cone cutouts, paper scraps, scissors, and glue. Also provide a mixture of two parts nonmentholated shaving cream and one part white glue, tinted as desired. A child glues a cone to a sheet of paper. Then she puts a dollop of the mixture on the paper above the cone and spreads it with her fingers until it resembles a scoop of ice cream. As she works, she repeats the phrase "ice-cold ice cream," emphasizing each $\bar{\imath}$/ sound. Then she cuts the paper scraps into small pieces and presses the resulting sprinkles onto the wet mixture. **Beginning sound** /$\bar{\imath}$/

Literacy Center

For each child, cut out a large uppercase *I*. Set out torn aluminum foil strips (icicles), waxed paper squares (ice cubes), and glue. A youngster picks an item and says its name, emphasizing the /$\bar{\imath}$/ sound. Then she glues the item to her letter cutout. She continues in the same way until she is satisfied with her work. **Letter-sound association**

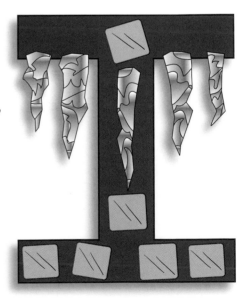

Games Center

For each player, label a lotto board with upper-case and lowercase *I*s. Label a corresponding number of milk caps to match the letters and also label a few with different letters. Place the caps in a bag. A student picks a cap. If the cap shows a lowercase or an uppercase *I,* he places it on a matching space. If it does not, he puts it back in the bag and the next child takes a turn. Play continues until each youngster fills his board. **Letter matching**

Gross-Motor Area

On a paved outdoor surface, use chalk to draw a multiscoop ice cream cone like the one shown. Label several scoops with the letter *I* and a few with different letters. Starting at the cone, a youngster hops on each scoop labeled *I* and over each scoop labeled with a different letter until she reaches the cherry. **Letter recognition**

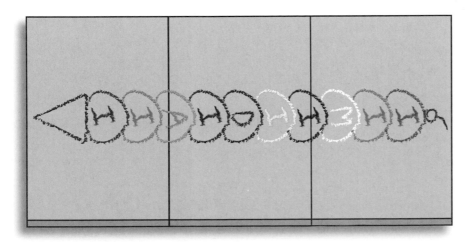

Fine-Motor Area

Label several foam cubes (ice cubes) with upper-case or lowercase *I*s. Place the cubes in an ice bucket or a plastic pail. Provide a pair of tongs and two cups, labeled as shown. A child uses the tongs to pick up each cube and place it in the appropriate cup. **Uppercase and lowercase letters**

Math Center

For this comparing-sets activity, make a copy of page 102 for each child. Label a letter card with both an upper-case and a lowercase *I,* making each letter a different color. Set out the card and a marker for each color used. A student refers to the card and uses the markers of the corresponding colors to circle the appropriate letters. She counts each uppercase *I* and then each lowercase *i* aloud and determines which set of letters has more and which has fewer. **Uppercase and lowercase letters**

Writing Center

Put a dollop of icing in a resealable plastic bag. Close the bag and reinforce the seal with packing tape. Display a large uppercase and lowercase letter *I*. A child rubs her hand across the bag to smooth out the icing. Then she uses her fingertip to write uppercase and lowercase *I*s in the icing, smoothing out the icing after writing each letter. **Letter formation**

Snack Center

Set out pretzel sticks, chocolate chips, and napkins. Display an uppercase and a lowercase letter *I*. A child arranges pretzel sticks on a napkin to make each letter, using a chocolate chip to dot the lowercase *i*. After he traces above the letters with his fingertip, he eats the letters! **Letter formation**

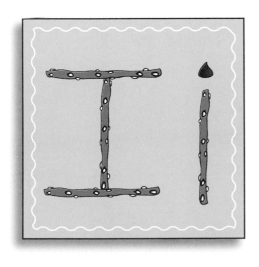

Fine-Motor Area

To make this jellyfish, set out a paper plate half, several crepe paper strips, markers, and tape. A child draws a face on the plate half. Then he tapes one end of each crepe paper strip to the straight edge of the plate half so it resembles a tentacle. As he works, he repeats the phrase *jolly, jiggling jellyfish,* emphasizing each /j/ sound. **Beginning sound /j/**

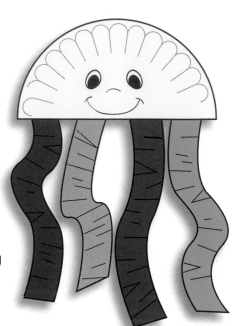

Art Center

Set out a large paper bread slice cutout, a container of purple paint (jelly), and a letter *J* sponge stamp. A youngster dips the sponge in the jelly and then presses it on the bread slice. She practices the letter *J* sound by saying /j/ each time she presses the sponge on the bread. **Letter-sound association**

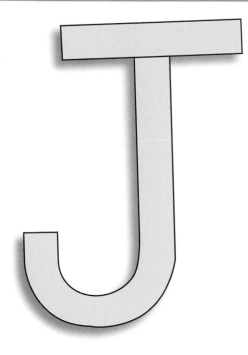

Use masking tape to make a few oversize *J*s on the floor. A student jumps along a letter, making the /j/ sound as he jumps. He continues in the same way with the remaining *J*s. **Letter-sound association**

Gross-Motor Area

Program a bag as shown. Place in the bag several cards labeled with *J* and a few labeled with different letters. Provide a large jingle bell. A child picks a card from the bag. If the card is programmed with a *J,* she jingles the bell. If it is not, she places it to the side. She continues in the same manner with each remaining card. **Letter recognition**

Sensory Center

Literacy Center

Set out an empty plastic jam or jelly jar labeled as shown. Place a supply of letter manipulatives nearby, making sure to include lots of *J*s. A youngster finds the *J*s and places them in the jar. **Letter recognition**

Sand Table

Label laminated jewel cutouts with letters, writing *J* on most. Hide the cutouts in the sand and place an empty jewelry box labeled with the letter *J* nearby. Also provide a small sifter. A child sifts the sand to find jewels. If he finds a jewel labeled with a *J,* he puts it in the box. If he finds a jewel labeled with a different letter, he returns it to the sand. **Letter recognition**

Centers From A to Z • ©The Mailbox® Books • TEC61277

Dramatic-Play Area

Place throughout the area a supply of cards programmed with either a *J* or a *j*. Also provide cleaning supplies such as those shown, a shirt labeled "Janitor," and two containers labeled as shown. A student puts on the shirt and, as she cleans, she places each card she finds in the corresponding container. **Uppercase and lowercase letters**

Writing Center

Put a dollop of jelly in a resealable plastic bag. Close the bag and reinforce the seal with packing tape. Display an uppercase and a lowercase *J*. A youngster uses her fingertip to practice writing uppercase and lowercase *J*s in the jelly, smoothing out the jelly each time she finishes writing a letter. **Letter formation**

Snack Center

Set out large round cookies, pretzel sticks, chocolate chips, triangle-shaped crackers, icing, paper plates, and plastic knives. To make a kitten, a youngster spreads icing on a cookie (head). Then he presses three chocolate chips (two eyes and a nose), pretzel sticks (whiskers), and two crackers (ears) into the icing. When his kitten is complete, he says, "Kitten, kitten! Time for a snack!" emphasizing each /k/ sound. **Beginning sound /k/**

Literacy Center

Cut out a copy of the picture cards from page 103 and place them face-down. Provide an apron with a front pocket (kangaroo pouch). A child puts on the apron; then she turns over a card and says the object's name and its beginning sound. If the object's name begins like *kangaroo,* she hops up and down and then places the card in her pouch. If it does not, she places the card to the side. She continues with each remaining card. **Beginning sound /k/**

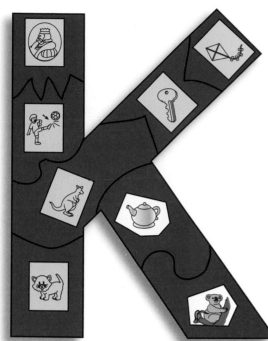

Puzzle Center

Puzzle-cut a large tagboard *K* to make several pieces. Label each piece with a picture of an object that begins with the /k/ sound. (If desired, use picture cards on page 103.) Store the pieces in a resealable plastic bag. A student removes the pieces from the bag and assembles the puzzle. As he works, he names the picture on each puzzle piece, emphasizing each /k/ sound. **For an added challenge,** provide a few puzzle pieces that do not fit the puzzle and are labeled with pictures that begin with different sounds. **Letter-sound association**

Art Center

Set out a construction paper kite cutout, a marker, tissue paper squares, glue, crepe paper, and tape. Also display a letter *K*. A youngster writes a large *K* on her kite. Then she crumples tissue paper squares and glues them along the lines of the letter. As she works, she repeats the phrase "*K* is for *kite*," emphasizing the /k/ sound. To complete her project, she tapes a length of crepe paper to the kite to make a tail. **Letter-sound association**

Water Table

Label several disposable cups with the letter *K* and a few with different letters. Place the cups in your empty water table and provide a small plastic kettle filled with water. A student takes a cup. If the cup is labeled with *K,* he pours a small amount of water in it. If the cup is labeled with a different letter, he removes it from the table. He continues with each remaining cup. **Letter recognition**

Literacy Center

Cut several candy kiss shapes from brown paper. Program most of the candy kisses with the letter *K* and the rest with different letters. Place the candy pieces letter-side down near a bowl labeled as shown. A child turns over a candy. If it is labeled with a *K,* she places it in the bowl. If it is labeled with a different letter, she leaves it faceup. **Letter recognition**

Set out two large door cutouts labeled as shown. Also provide key cutouts, each labeled with an uppercase *K* or a lowercase *k*. A student picks a key and places it on the appropriate door. He continues with each remaining key. **Uppercase and lowercase letters**

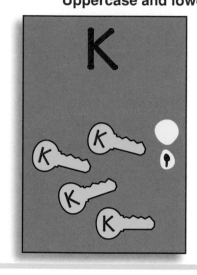

Set out a large paper plate, a sheet of yellow construction paper, scissors, glue, and a squeeze bottle filled with red paint (ketchup). A child cuts rectangles (french fries) from the paper and glues them to the plate. When she is satisfied with her work, she squeezes several ketchup *K*s onto the french fries. **Letter formation**

Games Center

To begin, Player 1 secretly hides a stuffed lamb in a designated area. Then Player 2 calls for the "little lost lamb," emphasizing each /l/ sound as she searches for the lamb. After she finds it, the youngsters switch roles to play another round. **Beginning sound /l/**

Gross-Motor Area

Place on the floor a large log cutout. On one side of the log, stack several pictures of objects, most of whose names begin with *L*. A child chooses a picture and names the object. If the object's name begins like *log,* he jumps over the log to place the picture on the other side. If the picture's name does not begin like *log,* he sets the picture aside. **Beginning sound /l/**

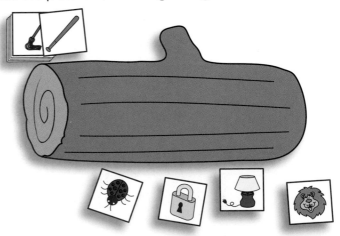

Centers From A to Z • ©The Mailbox® Books • TEC61277

Lion loves...

Literacy Center

Set out a class supply of the sentence starter from the bottom of page 101 along with paper, crayons, and glue. A child glues a sentence starter to the top of a sheet of paper. Below the sentence starter, he draws things that begin like *lion*. For an added challenge, help students label their drawings. **Letter-sound association**

Water Table

Use red and blue food coloring to tint the water lavender. Float a supply of foam letters in the water, making sure to include several *L*s. A child uses a ladle to scoop each *L* into a plastic bowl. For added fun, she chants, "I'm looking in the lavender water for *L*s" as she searches. **Letter recognition**

Gross-Motor Area

Use strips of masking tape to make a ladder on the floor. Set a stack of letter cards containing several cards labeled with *L* facedown nearby. A child stands at the bottom of the ladder and holds the card stack. He flips over the top card and reads the letter. If the card is labeled with an *L,* he moves to the next rung of the ladder. If not, he stays where he is. He continues until he reaches the top of the ladder. **Letter recognition**

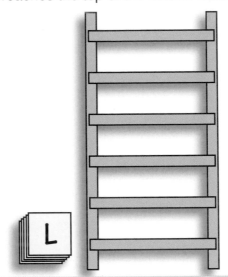

Literacy Center

Program a supply of leaf cutouts each with an uppercase or a lowercase *L.* Set the leaves near two large tree cutouts labeled as shown. A child reads the letter on each leaf and places it on its matching tree. **Uppercase and lowercase letters**

Use lemon and lime gelatin powders to scent yellow and green play dough, respectively. A child rolls the play dough into snakes and then uses the snakes to make several uppercase and lowercase *L*s. **Letter formation**

Play Dough Center

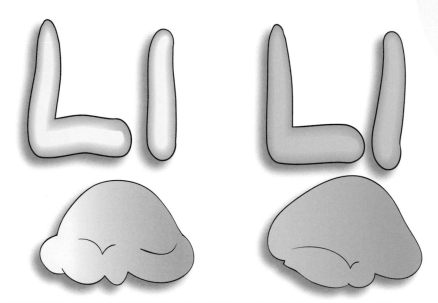

Set out a small leaf tracer, sheets of white construction paper, and crayons. A child uses the crayons to trace several leaves on the paper. In his best handwriting, he writes an *L* or *l* on each leaf. **Letter formation**

Fine-Motor Area

Mm

Literacy Center

Place in a container several objects or pictures of objects whose names begin with /m/. Add a few items whose names begin with different sounds as well. Display the container near a large moon-shaped cutout. A child puts each item whose name begins like *moon* on top of the cutout. **Beginning sound /m/**

Play Dough Center

Set out play dough, pipe cleaner pieces, and a laminated copy of page 104. A child molds dough into a mouse shape and adds a pipe cleaner tail. He moves the mouse along the *M,* from the mouse hole to the muffin. Then he pretends to have the mouse eat the muffin as he says, "Munch, munch, munch— /m/, /m/, good!" emphasizing each /m/ sound. **Letter-sound association**

Mouse Maze

Art Center

For each child, label the center of a sheet of construction paper with the letter *M*. Set out ink pads and a variety of rubber stampers whose names begin with the letter *M*. To make a marvelous piece of artwork, a youngster stamps the pictures on her paper, naming each picture she stamps. **Letter-sound association**

Dramatic-Play Area

Prepare a mock mailbox similar to the one shown and label it with the letter *M*. Store in a bag several envelopes labeled with *M* along with a few envelopes labeled with different letters. A student pretends to be a mail carrier and places each envelope labeled with the letter *M* in the mailbox. **Letter recognition**

Math Center

Label each section of a muffin tin with an uppercase *M*. Label a minimuffin tin in the same way with lowercase *m*'s. Label large and small paper baking cups with the corresponding letters. A child places each baking cup in the correct pan after confirming that the letters match. **Uppercase and lowercase letters**

Sensory Center

Fill a sensory table with white foam packing peanuts (snow). Hide in the snow mitten cutouts that are each labeled with either an uppercase *M* or a lowercase *m*. Set out a few pairs of real mittens and two containers labeled as shown. A youngster puts on a pair of mittens, finds each cutout, and places it in the corresponding container. **Uppercase and lowercase letters**

Centers From A to Z • ©The Mailbox® Books • TEC61277

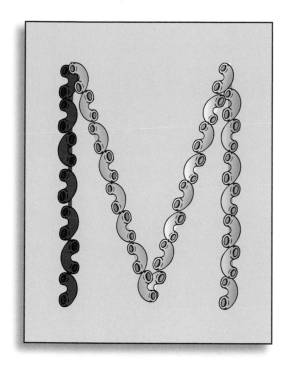

For each child, label a sheet of construction paper with a large letter *M*, making each line a different color. Set out glue and uncooked macaroni colored to match the lines. A student uses his fingertip to trace the letter. Then he glues the matching color of macaroni to each line. **Letter formation**

Fine-Motor Area

Set out construction paper, large hot dog and bun cutouts, pencils, condiment squeeze bottles filled with yellow paint (mustard) and labeled as shown, and glue. A youngster glues a hot dog and a bun to a sheet of paper. Next, she uses a pencil to practice writing *M*s on the paper. Then she uses a condiment bottle to squeeze mustard *M*s onto her hot dog. **Letter formation**

Art Center

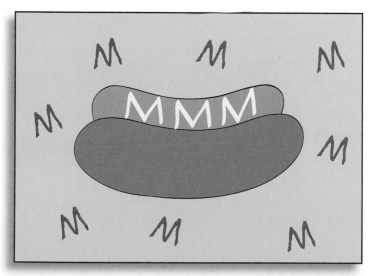

Literacy Center

Roll down the top of a paper grocery bag until it resembles a nest. Place in the nest items that begin with /n/, such as a newspaper, necklace, napkin, nickel, bag of noodles, and net. A child removes an item from the nest. She names the item, emphasizing the /n/ sound at the beginning of the word. She repeats the process for each item in the nest. **Beginning sound /n/**

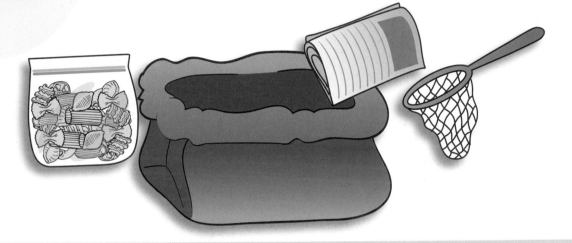

Math Center

To prepare for this patterning center, set out a tub of colorful noodles. A child arranges noodles to make a pattern. As she works, she says, "Nifty, nifty noodles," emphasizing each /n/ sound. After she repeats the pattern several times, she creates another pattern as time allows. **Beginning sound /n/**

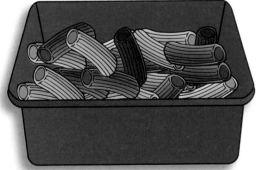

Sensory Center

Fill your sensory table with yellow paper shreds (hay). In the hay, hide several gray craft foam needles labeled with *N*s and a few labeled with different letters. Provide a basket labeled as shown. A youngster searches in the hay for needles. When he finds a needle labeled with the letter *N*, he puts it in the basket. When he finds a needle labeled with a different letter, he sets it aside. **Letter recognition**

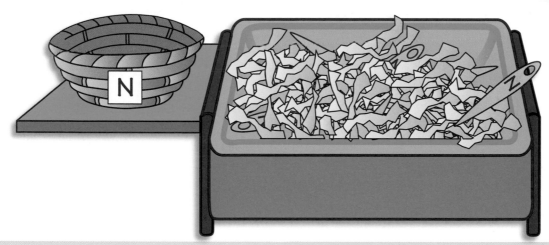

Games Center

For each twosome, cut out an enlarged copy of the squirrel pattern and two copies of the nut cards on page 105. The players stack the nut cards face-down near the squirrel. Then each player, in turn, takes a card and reads the letter. If the card is labeled with an *N,* the player "feeds" it to the squirrel. If the card is labeled with a different letter, she sets it aside. Play continues until the players have fed each *N* to the squirrel. **Letter recognition**

Gross-Motor Area

Place on the floor two plastic hoops labeled as shown. On each of several beanbags, attach a letter card labeled with an uppercase or a lowercase *N*. A child reads the letter on each beanbag and tosses it into the correct hoop. **Uppercase and lowercase letters**

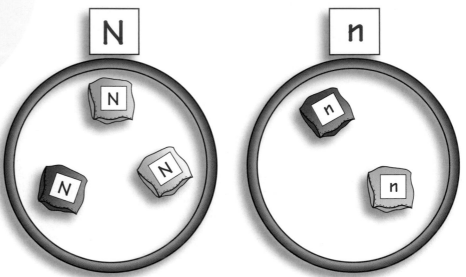

Literacy Center

Cut from poster board an extra-large uppercase and lowercase *N.* Set the cutouts near scissors and a supply of newspaper. A child finds uppercase and lowercase *N*s in the newspaper and cuts them out. Then he glues each one to its matching letter cutout. **Uppercase and lowercase letters**

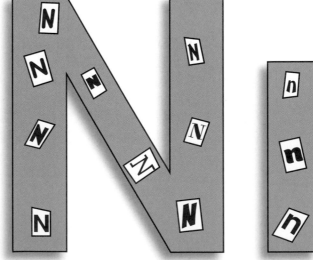

Centers From A to Z • ©The Mailbox® Books • TEC61277

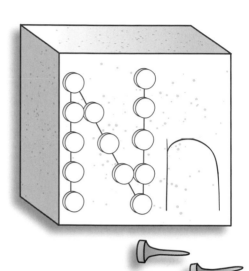

Write an uppercase and a lowercase *N* on a large foam block. Then set golf tees (nails) and a toy hammer nearby. A child gently taps the nails into the foam block along each letter. **Letter formation**

Fine-Motor Area

Post a list of words that begin with *N* along with matching pictures. Also set out stationary and note-cards. A youngster writes or dictates a note to a friend or family member using one or more words on the list. Then she adds an illustration to her note. **Initial consonant *n***

Writing Center

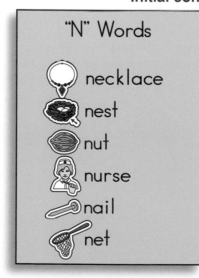

"N" Words

necklace
nest
nut
nurse
nail
net

I like my new necklace.

Literacy Center

Set out a pair of overalls or a cutout of overalls. Place near the overalls items or pictures of items that begin with the long /o/ sound, such as a paper oval, a packet of oatmeal, a picture of a ball going over a net, and a picture of an open door. Add a few items whose names begin with other sounds as well. A child puts each item whose name begins with the long /o/ sound on top of the overalls. **Beginning sound /ō/**

Art Center

Set out large construction paper ovals and shallow containers of paint. Place items for stamping the letter *O*—such as a cardboard tube, a foam pool noodle chunk, and a disposable cup—near the paint. A student dips one end of an object in paint and then presses it on an oval to make an *O*. As he works, he says, *"Oval begins with O!"* emphasizing each /ō/ sound. He continues making *O*s as time allows. **Letter-sound association**

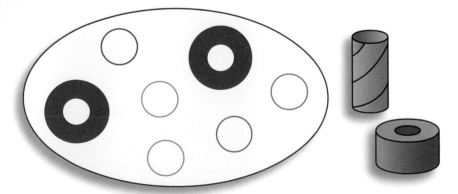

Centers From A to Z • ©The Mailbox® Books • TEC61277

Partially fill a plastic tub with dry oatmeal. Bury several letter *O* manipulatives and a handful of other letters in the oatmeal. Provide a slotted spoon and an empty oatmeal container labeled with the letter *O.* A youngster uses the spoon to dig for *O*s in the oatmeal. Each time she finds an *O,* she places it in the oatmeal container. When she finds other letters, she sets them aside. **Letter recognition**

Sensory Center

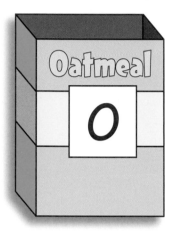 

Label several orange construction paper circles (oranges) with the letter *O* and a few with other letters. Place the oranges facedown on a tree cutout. A student turns over an orange. If it is labeled with the letter *O,* he leaves it on the tree. If it is labeled with another letter, he takes it off the tree and sets it aside. **Letter recognition**

Literacy Center

Writing Center

Make a copy of page 106 for each child. Label a card with an *O* and an *o*, making each letter a different color. Set out the card and a marker or crayon for each color used to label the card. A child refers to the card and uses the appropriate color of writing tool to trace each letter on his paper. **Uppercase and lowercase letters**

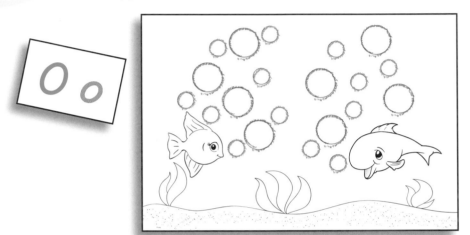

Gross-Motor Area

Set out two empty containers labeled as shown. A short distance away, place a supply of uppercase and lowercase letter *O*s made from pipe cleaners. A youngster takes an *O* and tosses it in the appropriate container. She continues with each remaining *O*. **Uppercase and lowercase letters**

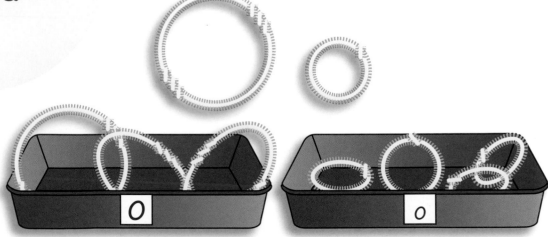

Centers From A to Z • ©The Mailbox® Books • TEC61277

For each child, label a paper square with an *O*. Provide self-adhesive hole reinforcers. To make an *O*, a student presses hole reinforcers along the letter. When he is finished, he uses his fingertip to trace (and feel) the shape of his textured letter *O*. **Letter formation**

Fine-Motor Area

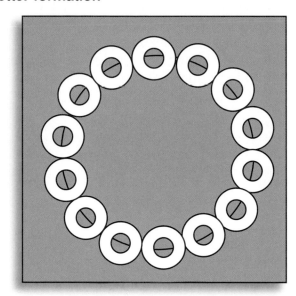

Partially fill a tray with moist sand. Set out a disposable cup and a tool for writing, such as an unsharpened pencil, a small wooden dowel, or a craft stick. A youngster presses one end of the cup in the sand several times, making letter *O* impressions. Then she uses a writing tool to trace the impressions. For an added challenge, after tracing the impressions, she uses a writing tool to write *O*s in the sand. **Letter formation**

Writing Center

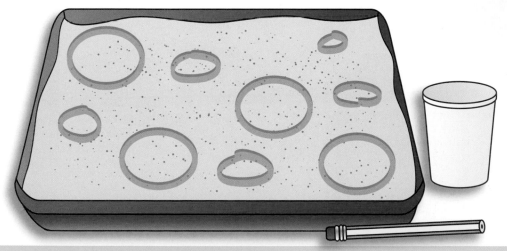

Pp

Art Center

Set out construction paper copies of the pig pattern on page 107 along with pink and purple bingo daubers. A youngster uses the daubers to stamp polka dots on her pig. As she works, she chants, "Pink and purple polka dots," emphasizing each /p/ sound. If desired, help youngsters cut out their pigs and glue them to construction paper puddles. **Beginning sound /p/**

Literacy Center

Place in a shopping bag several objects or pictures of objects whose names begin with /p/ and a few whose names begin with different sounds. Place the bag near a large pot and spoon. To make a batch of *P* soup, a child puts each item whose name begins with /p/ in the pot and then stirs the pretend soup. **Beginning sound /p/**

Centers From A to Z • ©The Mailbox® Books • TEC61277

Play Dough Center

Scent a batch of orange play dough with pumpkin pie spice. Set out the dough along with a small pie tin, a rolling pin, and a letter *P* cookie cutter. A youngster makes a pretend pumpkin pie. Then he gently stamps the letter *P* on top of his pie and says, *"P is for pumpkin pie,"* emphasizing each /p/ sound. **Letter-sound association**

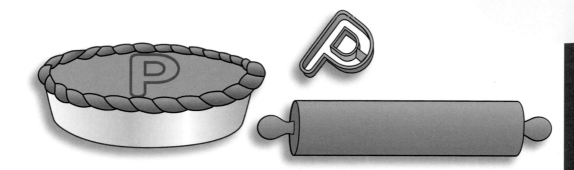

Literacy Center

Place facedown on a large cookie sheet (griddle) several craft foam pancakes labeled with *P* and a few labeled with different letters. Set out a spatula and a paper plate. A student uses the spatula to flip over a pancake. If the pancake is labeled with a *P*, she puts it on the plate. As she moves the pancake from the griddle to the plate, she says, *"P is for pancake,"* emphasizing each /p/ sound. She continues in the same way, making a stack of letter *P* pancakes. **Letter-sound association**

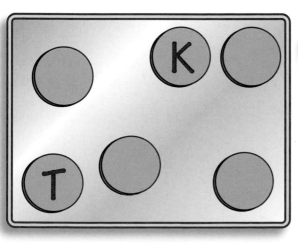

Sensory Center

Fill your sensory table with green paper strips (vines). Hide in the vines several green craft foam pea pods labeled with *P*s and a few labeled with different letters. Provide a plastic pail labeled as shown. A youngster pretends to go pea picking. When he finds a pea pod labeled with the letter *P,* he puts it in the pail. When he finds a pod labeled with a different letter, he sets it aside. **Letter recognition**

Games Center

Program a supply of pickle cutouts with the letter *P* and a few with different letters. Place the pickles in a plastic jar. A student sorts the pickles into two piles: those programmed with the letter *P* and those programmed with different letters. Then she places the pickles programmed with *P* in the jar. **Letter recognition**

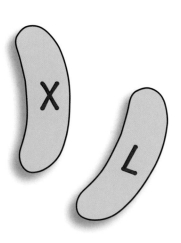

Centers From A to Z • ©The Mailbox® Books • TEC61277

Snack Center

Display the letter *P* and provide a bowl of pudding, craft sticks, paper plates, and plastic spoons. A child puts a dollop or two of pudding on his plate and then spreads the pudding with the craft stick. He uses the craft stick to write a *P* in the pudding and then smooths out the pudding. After writing the letter several times, he eats the pudding! **Letter formation**

Art Center

Set out tan construction paper circles (pancakes), small yellow paper squares (butter), paper plates, glue, and a squeeze bottle of glue mixed with maple syrup. A child glues a pancake to a plate and then glues butter to the pancake. Then she uses the squeeze bottle to make maple-scented *P*s on her pancake. **Letter formation**

Water Table

Float several rubber ducks in your water table. Provide a spray bottle filled with water. A child uses the spray bottle to squirt the ducks. Each time he squirts a duck, he says, "Quack, quack!" emphasizing the beginning sounds. **Beginning sound /kw/**

Literacy Center

Store several letter *Q* manipulatives in a bag. Add a few different letter manipulatives as well. Place the bag near a small quilt. A youngster picks a letter from the bag. If it is a letter *Q,* he places it on the quilt. If it is not, he sets the letter aside. He continues until the bag is empty. **Letter recognition**

Centers From A to Z • ©The Mailbox® Books • TEC61277

Program tagboard squares with the letter *Q*. Punch holes around the edges of each square; then tie one end of a length of yarn to each square. Set out the squares along with tape, pieces of yarn, and a squeeze bottle of glue. To make a quilt square, a student laces the yarn around the edge of a square. After he is finished lacing, he tapes the free end of the yarn to the square. To complete the project, he squeezes glue along the letter and presses yarn pieces on the glue. **Letter formation**

Fine-Motor Area

Set out different colors of paint, a large feather (quill) for each color, and a supply of paper. Also display a letter *Q*. A youngster dips the tip of a feather in paint and then uses it to write *Q*s on a sheet of paper, dipping the tip of the feather in the paint again as needed. **Letter formation**

Writing Center

Water Table

Add to your water table items such as colanders, strainers, sieves, and watering cans. Also provide a raincoat and rain hat. A child puts on the rainy day apparel and uses the rainmaking devices to create pretend rain. As she works, she sings this song, emphasizing each /r/ sound. **Beginning sound /r/**

(sung to the tune of "Twinkle, Twinkle, Little Star")

Raindrops, raindrops falling down,
Raindrops falling to the ground.
Raindrops falling fast and slow,
Raindrops falling head to toe.
Raindrops, raindrops falling down,
Raindrops falling to the ground!

Gross-Motor Area

Set out a colored and cutout copy of the action cards on page 108 and the props shown. A student takes a card and performs the designated action. As he performs the action, he repeats the action word, emphasizing the /r/ sound. He continues in the same way until he has used all the cards. **Beginning sound /r/**

Literacy Center

Place in a container several objects or pictures of objects whose names begin with /r/, along with a few items whose names begin with different sounds. Display the container near a large rainbow cutout. A youngster places each item whose name begins like *rainbow* on the cutout. **Beginning sound /r/**

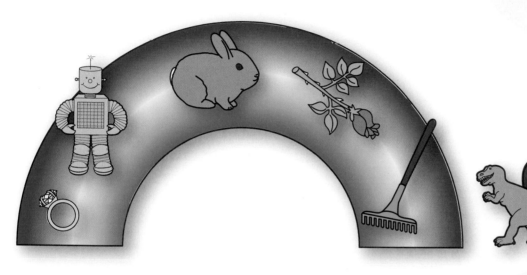

Fine-Motor Area

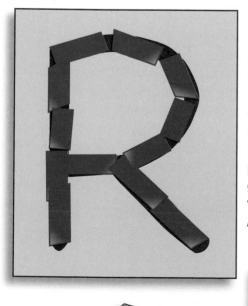

For each child, label a sheet of paper with an *R.* Set out small pieces of red ribbon and a squeeze bottle of glue. A student squeezes a thin line of glue along the lines of the letter and then presses ribbon pieces on the glue. As he works, he repeats the words *red ribbon,* emphasizing each /r/ sound. **Letter-sound association**

Math Center

For this one-to-one correspondence activity, program a sheet of paper with a cloud and raindrop outlines. Label several raindrop cutouts with an *R* and a few with different letters. Arrange the raindrops faceup. A child finds a raindrop with an *R* and places it on an outline. She continues matching one to one until each raindrop outline is covered by a raindrop programmed with an *R*. **Letter recognition**

Sand Table

Hide an assortment of letter manipulatives in the sand in your sand table, making sure to include several *R*s. Set out a container labeled as shown and a small toy rake. A youngster drags the rake through the sand, searching for *R*s. He places each *R* he finds in the container. **Letter recognition**

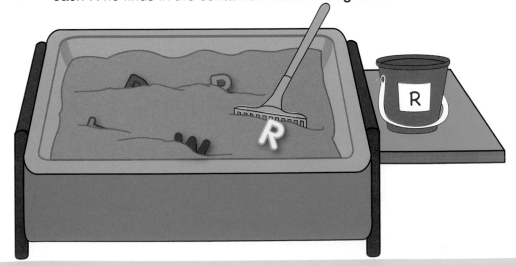

Provide red play dough, a dull pencil, and pieces of thin rope. A student flattens a lump of play dough and then uses the pencil to write the letter *R* in the dough. To complete the letter, she presses rope onto the pencil impression to form an *R*. **Letter formation**

Play Dough Center

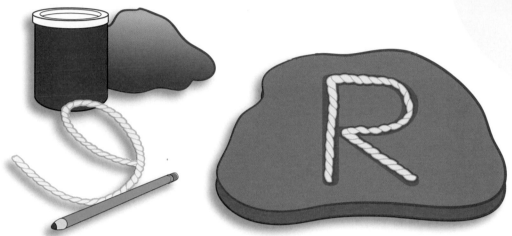

For each child, program a sheet of paper with a letter *R* outline. Set out glue and a container of red-tinted rice. A child uses a paint-brush to spread glue onto part of the outline. Then he uses his fingers to sprinkle rice on the glue. He continues in the same way until the outline is covered. **Letter formation**

Sensory Center

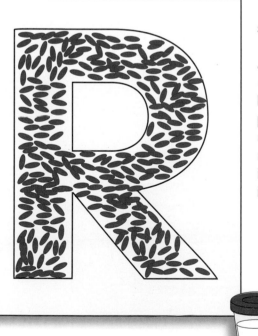

Water Table

Place a whisk or an eggbeater and several types of liquid soap near your water table. A child squeezes one or two squirts of soap in the water and then uses the whisk or eggbeater to make suds. While he is making suds, he says, "I am making soft soapy suds," emphasizing each /s/ sound. **Beginning sound /s/**

Gross-Motor Area

Pair sets of socks and fold them into balls. Set a laundry basket a few feet away from the socks. A child tosses the socks into the basket as she practices making the /s/ sound. **Beginning sound /s/**

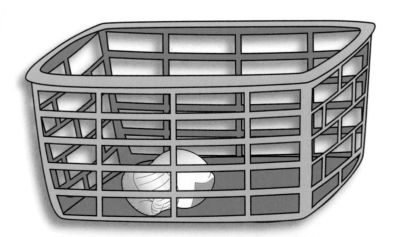

Literacy Center

Cut a large circle (sun) and several triangles (rays) from yellow paper. Label the sun with an *S*. On some of the rays, glue or draw pictures of objects that begin with /s/. On the other rays, glue or draw pictures of objects that begin with other sounds. Set out the sun and the rays. A child names the picture on each ray and places the rays with pictures that begin with the /s/ sound around the sun. **Letter-sound association**

Fine-Motor Area

Set out a class supply of *S* cutouts, a squeeze bottle of glue, and a shaker of silver glitter. A child squeezes drops of glue on an *S* cutout, practicing the /s/ sound as he works. To make silver spots, he sprinkles silver glitter on the glue and then shakes off the excess glitter. **Letter-sound association**

Games Center

Set out two bread-slice cutouts and a facedown stack of letter cards containing several Ss. To make a silly sandwich, each player, in turn, takes a card and reads the letter. If the letter is an S, he places the card on the bread slice. If the letter is not an S, he sets the card aside. After all the cards are sorted, the players use the second bread slice to complete the silly sandwich. **Letter recognition**

Literacy Center

Place green paper shreds (salad) in a large bowl. Then label several milk caps (salad toppings) with letters, making sure to label each of several caps with an S. Place the toppings in a smaller bowl. Set the salad and toppings near a pair of tongs. A child uses the tongs to pick up a topping and reads the letter. If the letter is an S, she adds the topping to the salad. If the letter is not an S, she sets the topping aside. **Letter recognition**

Place several seed cutouts labeled with either *S* or *s* in an envelope decorated as a seed packet. Place brown paper shreds (soil) in two containers labeled as shown. A child removes the seeds from the envelope and sorts them in front of their matching containers. Then she "plants" each set of seeds in its container. **Uppercase and lowercase letters**

Sensory Center

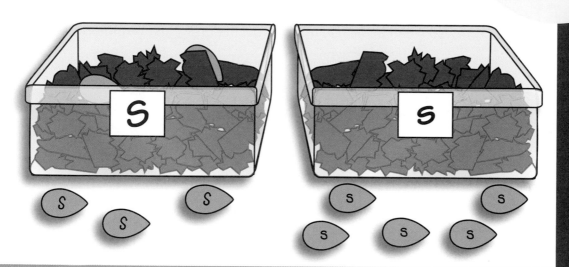

Set out a tagboard sock tracer, white paper, a white crayon, watercolors, and a paintbrush. A child traces the sock twice on a sheet of paper. Then she uses the white crayon to write several *S*s on each sock. She paints the socks with the watercolors to reveal the *S*s. When the paint is dry, she cuts out the socks. **Letter formation**

Art Center

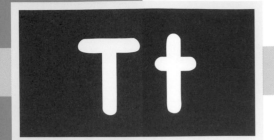

Art Center

Set out turtle body cutouts, turtle shell cutouts, and a stapler. A child draws a face on the head of a turtle cutout and draws pictures of things that begin like *turtle* on the turtle's body. Next, she decorates a shell. She staples her shell along the top of the turtle's body so it can be flipped up to reveal the drawings. **Beginning sound /t/**

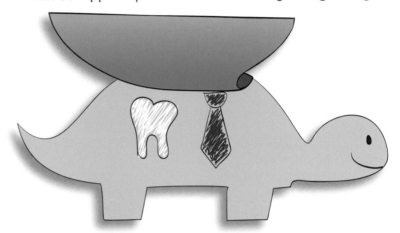

Gross-Motor Area

Attach a line of masking tape to the floor to make a tightrope. At one end of the tightrope, set several objects that begin with /t/ and a few objects that begin with other sounds. A youngster chooses an object that begins with /t/ and carries it across the tightrope, practicing the /t/ sound as she walks. She sets the object down at the opposite end and repeats the process with each remaining object that begins like *tightrope*. **Beginning sound /t/**

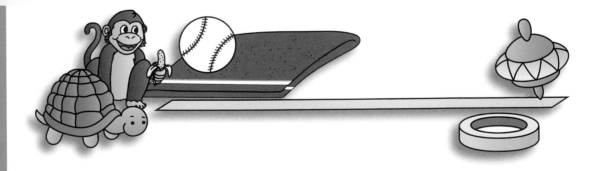

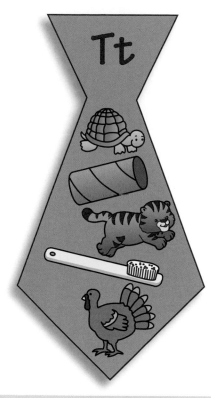

Place in a container several objects or pictures of objects whose names begin with /t/. Add a few items or pictures of items whose names begin with other sounds as well. Place the container near a large tie cutout labeled as shown. A child puts each item whose name begins like *tie* on the cutout. **Letter-sound association**

Literacy Center

Set out a class supply of *T* cutouts, construction paper scraps, and glue. A child tears the paper scraps and glues the pieces on the *T* cutout. As he works, he practices making the /t/ sound. **Letter-sound association**

Fine-Motor Area

Literacy Center

Set out a large tiger cutout or a stuffed tiger toy and place a tub of letter manipulatives (including several *T*s) nearby. A child chooses a letter manipulative. If the letter is a *T*, he places the letter on the tiger. If the letter is not a *T*, he sets it to the side. **Letter recognition**

Games Center

For this partner game, draw a tic-tac-toe board on a tagboard square. Then place five uppercase *T* cutouts and five lowercase *t* cutouts in a pile nearby. The players decide who will use uppercase *T*s and who will use lowercase *t*'s as game markers. Each player, in turn, places one of her game markers on the board. Play continues until one player has three of her letters in a row horizontally, vertically, or diagonally or all the spaces on the board have been covered. **Uppercase and lowercase letters**

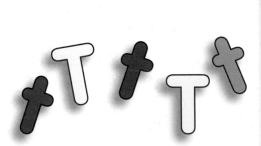

Centers From A to Z • ©The Mailbox® Books • TEC61277

Snack Center

To prepare, set out paper plates, toasted bread slices, and a squeeze bottle of jelly. A child squeezes jelly on the toast to make a *T* and a *t*. **Letter formation**

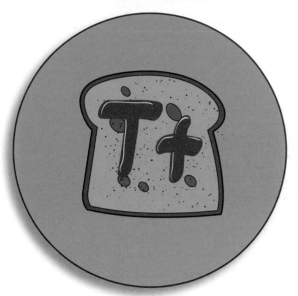

Fine-Motor Area

Squeeze toothpaste into a large resealable plastic bag and secure the top of the bag with tape. Set the bag near an unused toothbrush. A youngster spreads the tooth-paste with his hands. Then he uses the handle of the toothbrush to make several uppercase and lowercase *T*s in the toothpaste. **Letter formation**

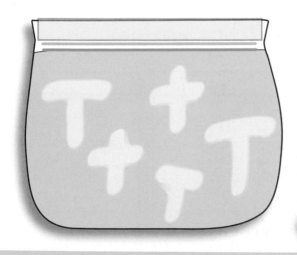

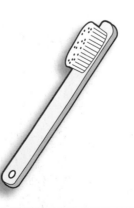

Uu

Games Center

Cut out a construction paper copy of the cards on page 109 and place them facedown. A child turns over two cards and names each picture, emphasizing each long /u/ sound. If the pictures match, he places them to the side. If not, he turns them back over and the next child takes a turn. Play continues in the same way until all the cards have been matched. **Beginning sound /ū/**

Gross-Motor Area

Cut out several large tagboard *U*s. Color and cut out enlarged copies of a unicorn, a unicycle, and a uniform card from page 109. Arrange the cards on the floor and make a tape line nearby. A student stands at the line and says, "*U* is for *[unicorn]!*" Then he attempts to toss a tagboard *U* onto the card that he named. **Letter-sound association**

Set out a large umbrella-shaped cutout. Provide several construction paper raindrops labeled with the letter *U* and a few labeled with different letters. A student finds each raindrop labeled *U* and puts it on the umbrella. **Letter recognition**

Literacy Center

Float in your water table several craft foam uppercase and lowercase *U*s. Place near the table two containers labeled as shown. Bend a pipe cleaner in half, twist the halves together, and then shape it into an uppercase *U*. A child uses the pipe cleaner to hook each craft foam *U* and place it in the correct container. **Uppercase and lowercase letters**

Water Table

Gross-Motor Area

Make an oversize masking tape *V* on the floor. Provide a toy vacuum cleaner. A youngster pushes the vacuum along the lines of the letter, practicing the initial sound of *vacuum* as she "cleans." **Letter-sound association**

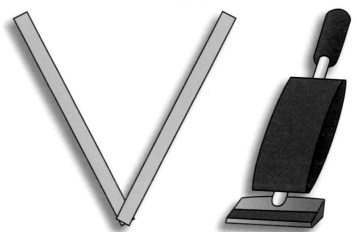

Fine-Motor Area

For each child, punch holes along a large letter *V* cutout; then tie a length of green yarn to one end. Set out glue and green construction paper leaves. A child laces the yarn through each hole and glues leaves to the letter so the yarn and leaves resemble a vine. When he is finished, he says, "That's a very nice vine!" emphasizing each /v/ sound. **Letter-sound association**

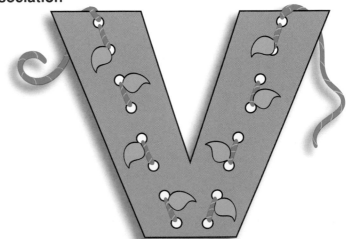

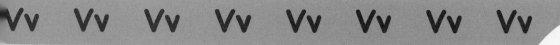

Near a large vase-shaped cutout, place several letter *V* manipulatives as well as a few different-letter manipulatives. A student finds each letter *V* and places it on the vase. **Letter recognition**

Literacy Center

Display the letter *V* and provide a bowl of vanilla pudding, rectangular vanilla-flavored wafers, large paper plates, and plastic spoons. A child places vanilla wafers on her plate to form the letter *V*. Then she spreads a small amount of vanilla pudding on top of each wafer. When she is finished, she eats her vanilla-flavored snack! **Letter formation**

Snack Center

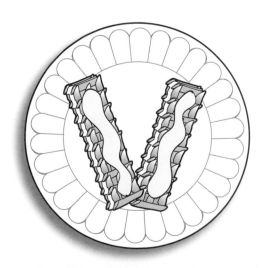

Literacy Center

Place in a container several objects or pictures of objects whose names begin with /w/, along with a few whose names begin with different sounds. Also draw waves on a large sheet of blue paper. Set out the paper and container. A child puts each item whose name begins with the /w/ sound on the water. **Beginning sound /w/**

Gross-Motor Area

Use masking tape to make an oversize *W* on the floor. Then draw a large dot on each point as shown. Standing at the beginning of the letter, a youngster wiggles her body down to the floor and then back up again, saying, "Wiggle, wiggle, wiggle," as she performs the action. Then she walks along the line of the letter, saying, "Walk, walk, walk," until she reaches the next dot, where she stops and wiggles up and down again. She continues in the same way along each line of the letter. **Letter-sound association**

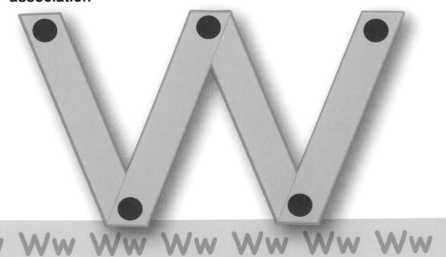

Art Center

Make student copies of page 110 on light blue construction paper. Set out the papers, a letter *W* stamper, and a blue stamp pad. A student repeatedly stamps *W*s around the walrus so they resemble waves. As he works, he sings about Wally the Walrus. **Letter-sound association**

(sung to the tune of "The Mulberry Bush")

Wally the Walrus is making waves,
Making waves, making waves.
Wally the Walrus is making waves
In the wonderful water!

Sensory Center

Fill the table with potting soil. Hide in the soil several craft foam worms labeled with *W* and a few labeled with different letters. Provide garden gloves, a small plastic shovel, and a container labeled as shown. A child digs a worm from the soil. If it is labeled with *W,* she puts it in the container. If it is labeled with a different letter, she sets it aside. **Letter recognition**

Games Center

For this partner game, label eight jumbo craft sticks with the letter *W*. Also label four craft sticks with different letters. Place the sticks facedown. In turn, each child picks a craft stick. If it is labeled with *W*, he places it in front of him to begin to form a *W*. If it is not, he returns the stick to its facedown position. Play continues until each child uses four craft sticks labeled with a *W* to form a *W* as shown. **Letter recognition**

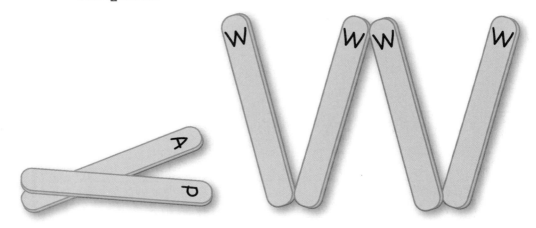

Literacy Center

Draw a simple spider on each of a several blank cards. Label some of the cards with an uppercase *W* and the remaining cards with a lowercase *w*. Draw two large web outlines and label them as shown. Set out the webs and stack the cards facedown nearby. A student takes a card and places it on the appropriate web. She continues with each remaining card. **Sorting uppercase and lowercase letters**

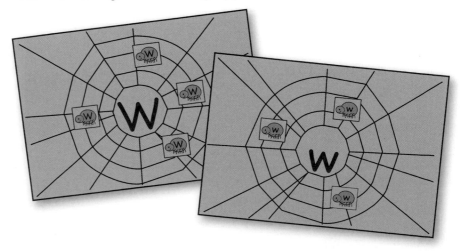

Play Dough Center

Set out pink watermelon-scented play dough, green play dough, and a craft stick. Also display a *W*. A youngster molds the dough to make a watermelon slice. Then he uses the craft stick to write *W*s on the watermelon. **Letter formation**

Snack Center

Provide a cooked waffle, a paper plate, and squeeze bottles filled with toppings such as jelly and syrup. Display a *W*. A child takes a topping of her choice and squeezes the letter *W* onto her waffle. After tracing the letter just above the topping with her finger, she eats her waffle. **Letter formation**

Centers From A to Z • ©The Mailbox® Books • TEC61277

Art Center

Display actual X-rays or pictures of X-rays for a child to study. Also provide black paper, white chalk, animal and people templates, and facial tissue. A child traces a template on the paper. Then he draws chalk details so the tracing resembles an X-ray. He gently wipes the chalk details with a tissue to create a shadowy effect. As he works, he sings the song below. **Beginning sound /ks/**

(sung to the tune of "The Farmer in the Dell")

It's X-ray art today.
It's X-ray art today.
Heigh-ho, don't you know?
It's X-ray art today!

Math Center

For this patterning activity, label a paper strip with an *AB* pattern of upper-case and lowercase *X*s. Then make a duplicate strip and cut between the letters to make individual letter cards. A child repeats the *AB* pattern by matching the letter cards to the original strip. **Letter matching**

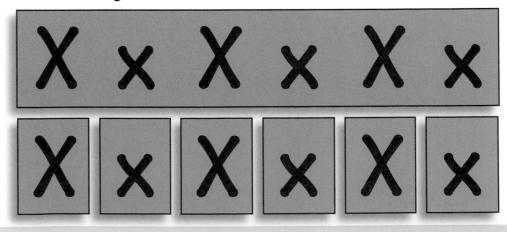

Post the letter *X* and provide play dough, small rolling pins, and an assortment of lace strips cut into equal lengths. A youngster rolls out a lump of dough. He presses two pieces of lace on the dough to make an *X.* Then he removes the lace to reveal a lovely *X* imprint. **Letter formation**

Play Dough Center

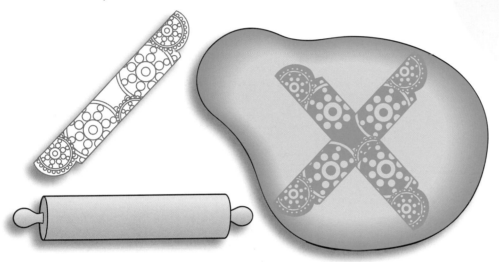

Set out paper plates, plastic knives, bagel halves, cream cheese, and a squeeze bottle of jelly. A child spreads cream cheese on a bagel half. Then she squeezes jelly on the bagel to make the letter *X.* **Letter formation**

Snack Center

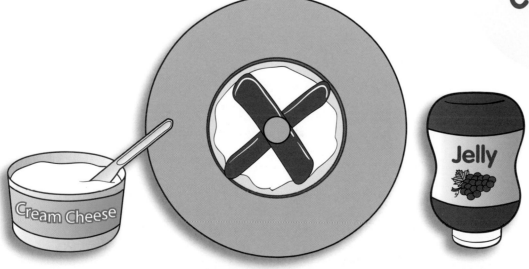

Snack Center

Set out a paper plate, a crème-filled cookie, and a length of shoestring licorice for each child. A child wraps a length of licorice string around the crème filling so it resembles a yo-yo string. As he works, he says, "A yummy yo-yo snack!" emphasizing each /y/ sound. **Beginning sound /y/**

Art Center

For each child, cut out a tagboard letter *Y.* Set out different lengths of yellow yarn and glue. A youngster glues yarn to her cutout, decorating it as desired until it is covered with yarn. As she works, she says, "Yay for yellow yarn!" emphasizing each /y/ sound. **Letter-sound association**

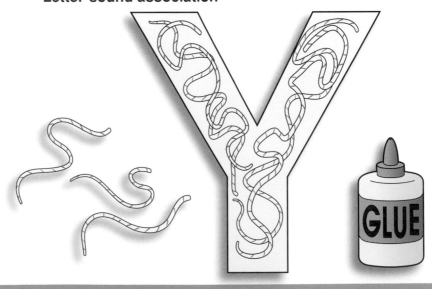

Centers From A to Z • ©The Mailbox® Books • TEC61277

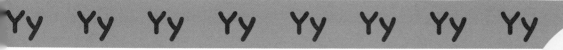

Literacy Center

Cut a supply of fried egg shapes from white craft foam and draw a yellow yolk on each. Label each yolk with either an uppercase *Y* or a lowercase *y*. Store the eggs in a frying pan. Place near the pan a spatula and two paper plates labeled as shown. Using the spatula, a student removes each egg from the pan and places it on the appropriate plate. **Uppercase and lowercase letters**

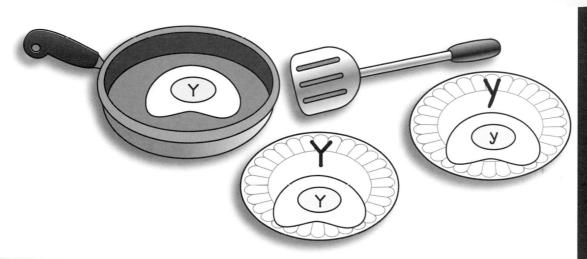

Writing Center

Put several spoonfuls of yogurt in a resealable plastic bag. Close the bag and reinforce the seal with packing tape. Display a large letter *Y*. A child rubs his hand across the bag to smooth out the yogurt. Then he uses his fingertip to write *Y*s in the yogurt, smoothing out the yogurt after writing each letter. **Letter formation**

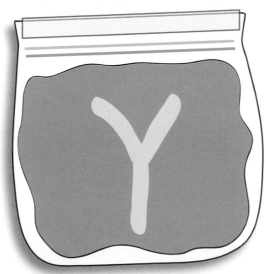

Fine-Motor Area

Set out several items with zippers, such as coats, cosmetic bags, and purses. A youngster zips and unzips the zippers while practicing the /z/ sound. **Beginning sound /z/**

Gross-Motor Area

Attach a large masking tape *Z* to the floor. Set several toy vehicles nearby. A little one drives a vehicle along the *Z* while he says, "I am zoom, zoom, zooming along," emphasizing each /z/ sound. **Letter-sound association**

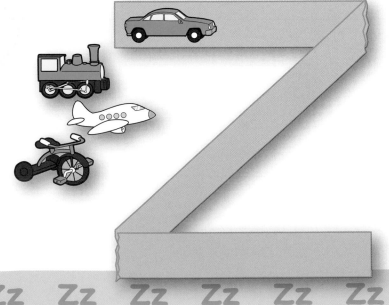

Art
Center

For each child, label a 12" x 18" sheet of construction paper as shown. Set out the programmed sheets, copies of the head and body patterns from page 111, crayons, markers, scissors, and glue. A child colors and cuts out the heads and bodies. To make a zany zoo, she glues the heads and bodies to the paper, pairing each head with a different animal's body. **Letter-sound association**

Art Center

A Zany Zoo

Place black crayons or markers near a class supply of copies of page 112. A youngster writes uppercase and lowercase *Z*s on the zebra's body to make stripes. **Letter formation**

Writing Center

Aa **Alligator Patterns**
Use with "Math Center" on page 5.

TEC61277

TEC61277

Aa **Acorn Pattern**
Use with "Games Center" on page 6.

Aa **Ant Pattern**
Use with "Literacy Center" on page 7.

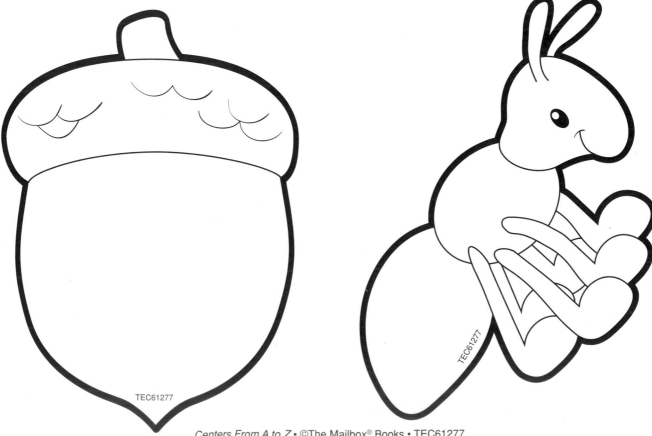

TEC61277

TEC61277

Centers From A to Z • ©The Mailbox® Books • TEC61277

Beginning Sound Picture Cards
Use with "Games Center" on page 9.

Bb

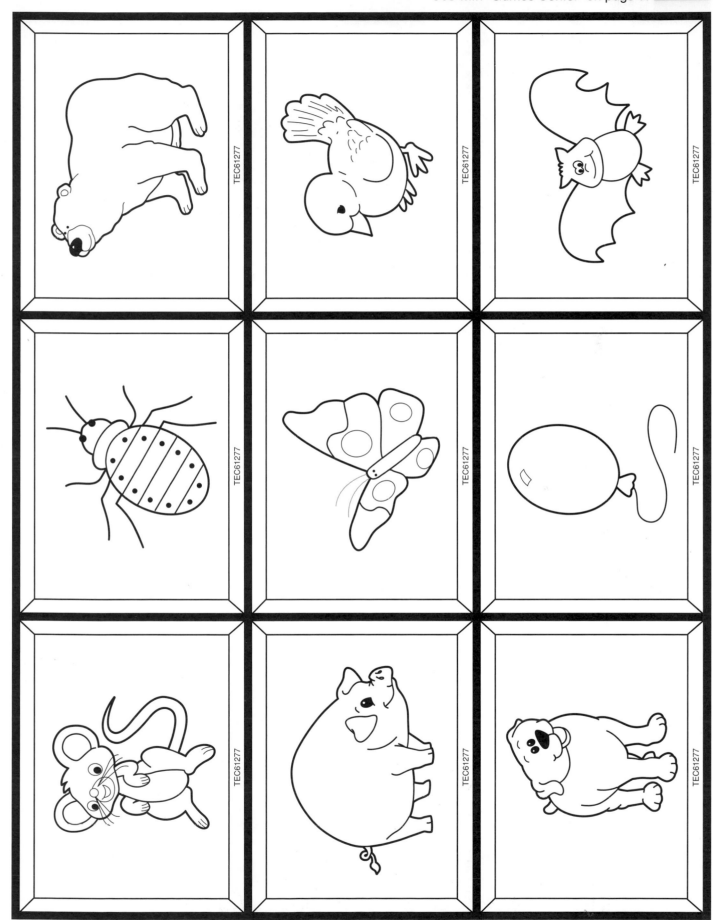

TEC61277

TEC61277

D Is for *Dog*

Note to the teacher: Use with "Literacy Center" on page 18.

99

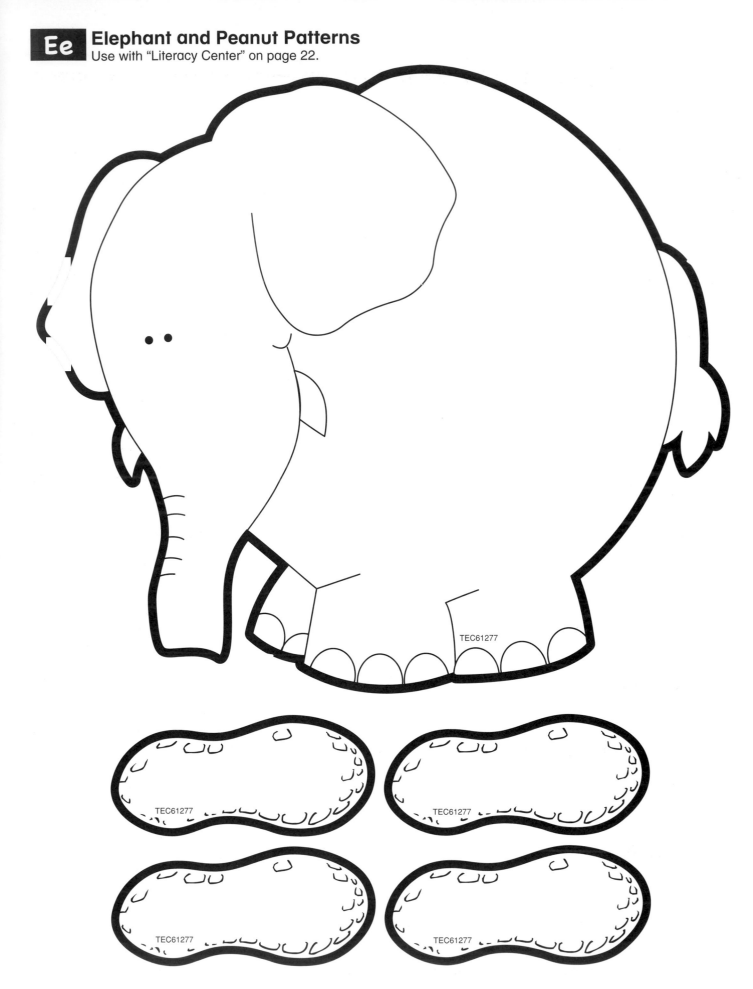

TEC61277

TEC61277

TEC61277

TEC61277

TEC61277

Centers From A to Z • ©The Mailbox® Books • TEC61277

TEC61277

TEC61277

TEC61277

TEC61277

TEC61277

TEC61277

TEC61277

TEC61277

TEC61277

Sentence Starter
Use with "Literacy Center" on page 49.

Lion loves...

TEC61277

I Spy the Letter *I*

P	I	O	m
i	A	I	S
c	I	G	i
I	F	i	Z
O	I	I	d

Note to the teacher: Use with "Math Center" on page 38.

Beginning Sound Cards: *K* **Kk**

Use with "Literacy Center" on page 44 and "Puzzle Center" on page 45.

TEC61277

TEC61277

TEC61277

TEC61277

TEC61277

TEC61277

TEC61277

TEC61277

TEC61277

Mouse Maze

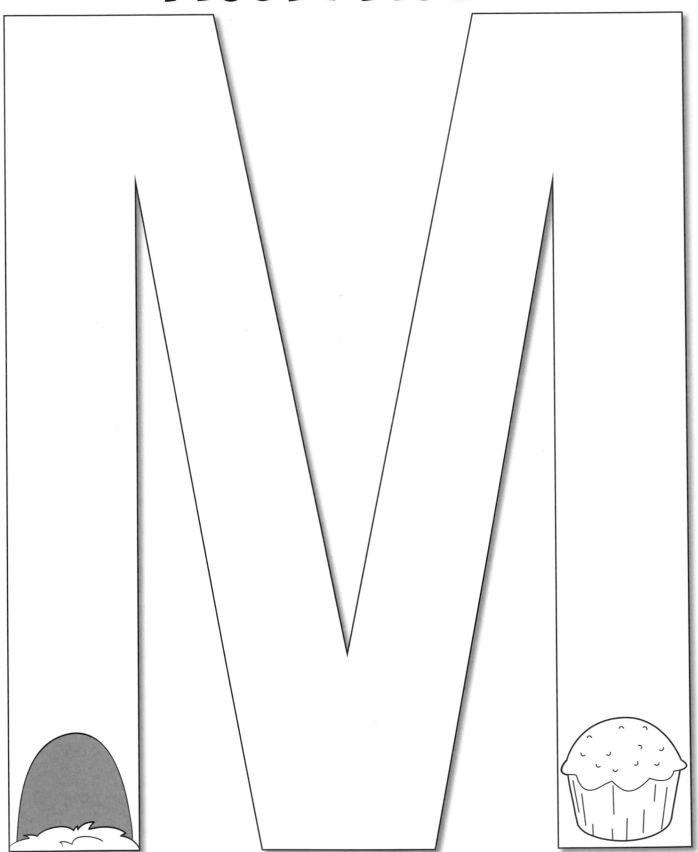

Centers From A to Z • ©The Mailbox® Books • TEC61277

Note to the teacher: Use with "Play Dough Center" on page 52.

Centers From A to Z ©The Mailbox® Books • TEC61277

Note to the teacher: Use with "Writing Center" on page 62.

Note to the teacher: Use with "Art Center" on page 64.

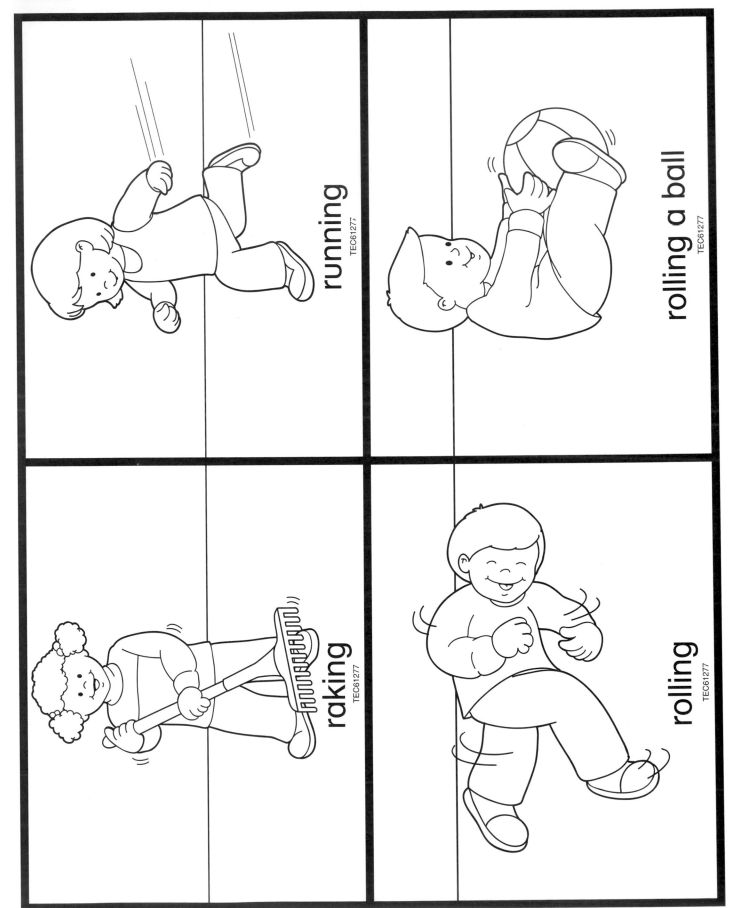

running

rolling a ball

raking

rolling

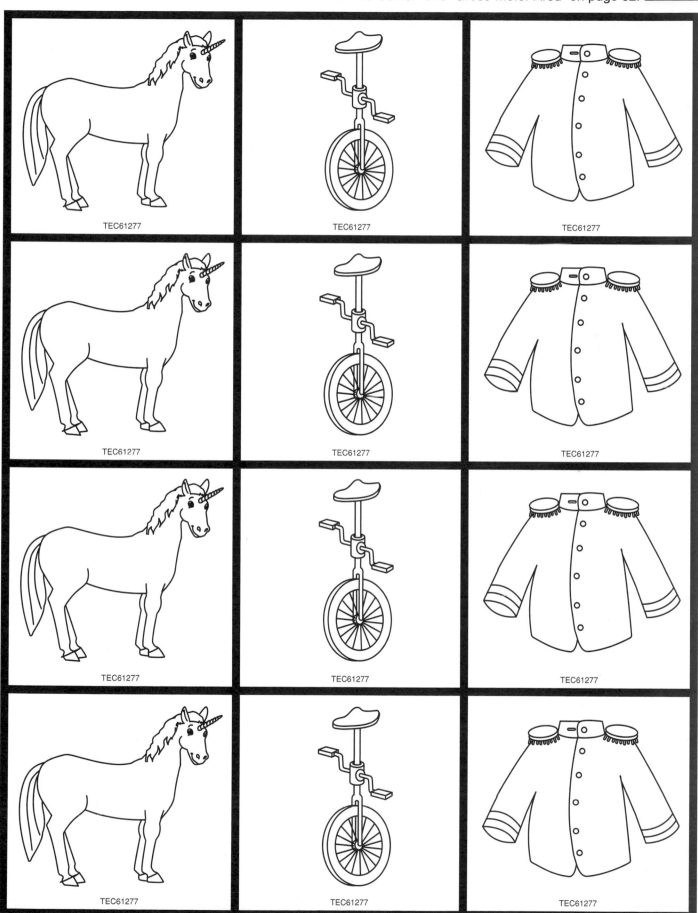

TEC61277

TEC61277

TEC61277

TEC61277

TEC61277

TEC61277

TEC61277

TEC61277

TEC61277

TEC61277

TEC61277

TEC61277

Centers From A to Z • ©The Mailbox® Books • TEC61277

Note to the teacher: Use with "Art Center" on page 87.

TEC61277

Centers From A to Z • ©The Mailbox® Books • TEC61277

Note to the teacher: Use with "Writing Center" on page 95.